Isolato

Poems by Larissa Szporluk

Isolato

UNIVERSITY OF IOWA PRESS   Ψ   *Iowa City*

University of Iowa Press, Iowa City 52242

Copyright © 2000 by Larissa Szporluk

Printed in the United States of America

Design by Richard Hendel

http://www.uiowa.edu/~uipress

Printed on acid-free paper

Library of Congress Cataloging-in-Publication Data

Szporluk, Larissa.

    Isolato: poems / by Larissa Szporluk.

       p.   cm.—(The Iowa poetry prize)

   ISBN 0-87745-704-2 (pbk.)

    I. Title. II. Series.

PS3569.Z6617 2000

811'.54—dc21   99-056176

00 01 02 03 04 P 5 4 3 2 1

FOR MY MOTHER & CARLO

CONTENTS

I.

One Thousand Bullfrogs Rejoice 3

Hatch No. 2 4

Deer Crossing the Sea 5

Leaving the Eccentric 6

Isolato 8

Trapeze 9

Givers and Takers 10

Faire Faire 12

Vertigo 14

II. SEVEN MARIA

Mare Desiderii 17

Mare Imbrium 18

Mare Orientalis 19

Mare Nubium 20

Mare Fecunditatis 21

Mare Frigoris 22

Mare Incognito 23

III.

Doppelgänger 27

Meteor 28

Median Strip 29

Eidola 31

Realm of the Fern 32

Elsewhere 34

Platonic Year 36

Homogeny 37

Jack and the Beanstalk 38

IV.

Triage 41

Chiaroscuro 43

Amusia 44

The Pearl of Great Price 46

Siege Piece 47

Pathogen 49

Eohippus 50

The Unforeseen 52

Malady of the Bird 55

ACKNOWLEDGMENTS

AGNI: "Pathogen," "Eohippus," "Isolato," "Siege Piece"

Green Mountains Review: "Deer Crossing the Sea" (also selected for
   Best American Poetry 1999 and *The Best of Beacon Press Anthology*)

Idaho Review: "Realm of the Fern," "Jack and the Beanstalk,"
   "Vertigo"

The *Journal*: "Meteor," "The Pearl of Great Price," "Givers and
   Takers"

Kenyon Review: "Faire Faire," "Homogeny," "Amusia," "Trapeze,"
   "Eidola," "Leaving the Eccentric" (a winner of the 1999
   International Poetry Competition, sponsored by the W. B. Yeats
   Society)

Michigan Quarterly Review: "Platonic Year"

Mississippi Review: "Seven Maria" (winner of the 1998 MR Prize)

The New Young American Poets, Southern Illinois University Press:
   "Triage"

Parnassus: "Median Strip"

Pleiades: "Triage," "Chiaroscuro," "Hatch No. 2"

Sonora Review: "One Thousand Bullfrogs Rejoice"

Special thanks to Rona Jaffe and the Rona Jaffe Foundation for the
grant that enabled me to write the poems, as well as to the Witter
Bynner Foundation, Kathleen Dixon, Arlene Spoores, Askold
Melnyczuk, Rosa O., Heidi J. Poon, and the anonymous judges
who picked this.

i.

It is dark inside the body, and wet,
and double-hearted. There are so many ways
to go, and not see, and lose
the feeling of the thread, which was alleged
to be invisible, and lose the man,
the fast Athenian, to someone with less rootage,
and never reach the fabled center,
afraid that if you did, you would find the hybrid,
not the hero, beautiful.

If you want to jump ahead,
Chapter Two just tells you how you erred
in Chapter One, taking his hand first
and being honest. Chapter Three says never mind,
you won't get another chance
to guide him. No one loves a volunteer.
No one loves a savior.
Chapter Four is set along the shore
where you are hiding, where life outside you
changes surface hourly.
Chapter Five: A skeleton is tangled
in a hyacinth. Their intimate clutch,
only for a minute, weirds you.
Tide is always bringing those reminders.
But here you keep in tune with rhythmic raging.
You open like a mussel made of gold
to anything in want of shelter,
anything with devious or laudable intentions.
Chapter Six. You open like a song
and bellow in the ear of second guessing.

Can't see a thing for the snow,
its rabid, haywire blowing,
something bigger than us
on a binge, plucking, skinning,
boning, the lie in my heart,
two wrongs make a right,
a parachute never unfolding.
Can't see my ex in his bright
existence, new live-in woman,
new business. See only
paths to a fairy tale castle,
a kiss after too much sleep.
See only late orange light
emanate up from old corn,
the way it covered your hands
as they caught it on film,
catch-as-catch-can. Good luck
in your loving endeavors, good
luck and godspeed. Forget
it was ours, kicking in water,
alive but unborn; forget I was
young in the brush-fire heat
and couldn't have known
it would bore through my shell
like a worm. See only Psyche
sort mountains of grain
with swift ant assistants.
Hear this one little chicken
talk about falling, but pay it
no heed. It hasn't come out yet.

It won't feel a thing.

Many things were like sleep,
wholly in the power of the forest,
the deep middle, deep shiver, deep shade,
from which many things ran, unawake,
in search of new mountains to graze,
covered in flowers, *my love, I am sick*,
or covered in snow, pink with algae,
in search of impossible light
made of water, whose sapphire waves
swathed their heads, *you were only a dream*,
as they swam out to meet it, kicking their hooves,
no longer breathing, because no one
or nothing can quit once the body gets wind
of an eden—the promise of nectar
haunts them forever, the shore pecked out
of their eyes, and there, in its stead,
something greater to catch,
a scent that would paralyze God.

The queenfish visits the spring
every spring, and she does it alone,
carried away from her silvery coast,
the blue drum region, carried away
by the aerial ocean above,
the dipping and rising, sidling along
saddles of thawing mountains,
thrashing through caribou tracks,
past dens of bears, exposing herself
to countless dangers, because of a whim
to be in the iciest possible
water, up to her eyes in the highest
spring, spring on the fringe of fish
civilization, spring where the king,
who loves her, lives, year after year,
for this single visit, the look of pain
on his outer face as he remembers
he should eat her. That's when the queen
takes her leave, flapping her battered
tail, slipping her body under. That's when
the one who loves her screams,
sharding the spring with manic octaves
(like bells of mules setting hills
ringing with each beating)—what else
can they do but follow its law
in wonder, the law of the sun
which burns, pulling the world to it,
the paradox of equinox, when light
and dark, and less and great, are all
the same, and every answer

strings its question up in space:
Are blood and love just things that run,
and if they're not, do they belong
to what they are, or to the place
they're running to or from, and what
if that's the point of life, to turn
your back into your front
and mount the beast again?

questions

essence

The ox is slow but the earth is patient.
The ox is in a war
of many tiers but no engagement,
like folds within a bellows
that broke from the accordion
(war to be alone in a shiftless wind
that does not answer,
war to be the only
child in existence, even frozen,
be the only sound that plows the only land,
and as the only one,
be dumb to all remembrance
of how small or strong or round
it ever was, how much work there is
undone, how long it's been
since any form of water has come down,
all thought about the whip,
how sharp it is against the moving bone,
all gone).
The earth is patient in this war,
knowing binds and chains
enflame the skin, and skin, like soft terrain,
loosens into freedom for the thorn,
and the thorn, squeezing from the tissue
like a devil or a leech,
bleeds into an almost touching song.

war

knowledge

power

body — "skin"

To float you must float from within.
You must not feel attached

as you brush past the body you loved,
an arm past an arm, an almost weightless vapor.

Don't ask questions anymore. Don't hear
his seismic voice. Fractures thread the floor;

time will energize their creep
until you're caving through his ceiling.

It's all a matter of containment,
held-in breath, the hidden table. Keep in mind

that dreaming up means waking down,
so keep your swing in limbo. Don't aim high:

Where air turns thin, the ear tears open
with a secret's restless heat,

surrendering its recess—the details of explosion
fizzling in a tree, remembered now and then,

but not so well, by something on and off,
like fireflies—when pressure mounts beneath it.

Father from afar,
where you have touched her,
you are not:

Almost a gush
as she opens up, famously loud,
inhaling the sky

and seminal dust
and man-made fly. Almost a gush
as you reel her out

and drop her on a pile.
One is a giver,
another a taker, life of fire.

Now your fingers,
quickly skillful, chop her up;
can't they tell her

from the captured,
lying stiffly on a platter,
torsos only,

grilled and blackened?
Wherever her mind is
(with the gutstuff, in the bucket,

floating homeward
without bonework), it's losing
10   focus, kindling inward,

winding down.
Trees ripple through her
severed fantail; aurora shadows

flail each eye.
Aren't you tickled, father, tackler,
to find her still alive,

find her bobbing,
like a fraction, top by bottom,
multiplied? Almost a gush

as partial daughter
loiters on the waist-high water,
flirting, gurgling,

words like tinsel,
Take me with you, I forgive you —
final shimmer, final bite.

It comes from eternity,
from its depths, its planes,
the little gift called time,
and enters what is ours,
to be our time. The lamb
could see the panorama
from the hilltop, if it tried,
but like time, it looks down,
to see the past it ate.
Time sees only time.
(The closer, not the greater,
thing from which it's made.)
The brain, bred in darkness,
sends dark waves, and wind
that builds inside the gland
blows cold brain, knowing
nothing of the soul that still
contains them—time, wind,
brain, knowing nothing of
what made them. The April
stream will feel itself alive
compared to land and thank
the moving sky, not the god
from whom the sky is made.
I tried to look around to find
the love from which I came,
but I was young, and looking
down, found your perfect
human face, and couldn't
see how mean it was,

how mean it grew in time,
squeezed of all eternity,
of depths, of planes, of eyes,
a barn whose subtle sink
runs an inch or two a year,
until its door is full of earth
and the wind cock pinned.

Sing now.
Sing from on high, high roof
you're afraid of
losing. Sing yourself into
a tiny blue worm,
maybe no eyes,
squeezing its mite
through a tinier
passage, maybe no
outlet, maybe
no light, maybe you'll never
ever find light,
and the stars that you think
in a world of height
there should be
aren't even stars, only actors
that swing in the dark
like paper lanterns
and don't serve as guides
as you peer from the edge
at the people below
without nets;
they don't know who you are,
but they're waiting
in droves
for your butterfly nerves
to tuck in their tails
and fold.

ii. *seven maria*

What is a crescent?

—*The moon has cut itself up.*

JEAN PIAGET,

The Child's Conception of the World

Maria (or "seas") are great dark plains on the moon's surface.

Turn to the source and feel
hoar steal off
your own monotonous vista,

moistening the walls
of lunar rock and silence
that keep your senses even.

June summons June across the planet;
the sun this year is silver,
just a sliver in your eyes.

Maybe you can live
in full aversion. Maybe you can limn
the far side of the moon.

But some night God is going to come
way up here and find you
erotically divided,

moving like two swans,
one with a slight lead, the other
with a cache of food.

You'll hear aviary noises
flee the dark blue corridor
He's pouring through. A warm hate

will loosen in your throat:
Don't speak, you'll motion to Him,
None of us can face it.

The plants have gone to witchcraft,
floripondium, owl-tongue, cananga.
She scatters the ribs, the wind, the roads,
increasing her means of isolation.
What cuts across the night for coitus
storms her without warning,
pinning her down. It's the washing
away of her heart on another morning,
the residual body's lost consent,
that seeps into the hills like poison.
After so many spells, the only language
is the fire of a person. Then comes a time
when the mouth won't even close,
and the dirt lies quiet at the bottom.

If the husband cheats, he does it
with the eastern portion of his heart,
if his heart is there at all. And like the sea
that dried up long before we knew a sea was there
at all, he does it with perfume,
a lithe and slimy youth, an aromatherapeutic
pheromone, *How old did you say you were?*
And he does it on a wall,
because a wall involves a risk,
a pain that won't forgive him when it's done,
a wall that stands immune,
long after he is gone, to how he fell,
a Humpty Dumpty in his coarse and rapid movements,
What a beautiful belt—
who jerked too much and splat
into a cleft. And what did the girl do,
small beside the peaks that frill the border,
small to the extreme, a craterlet,
exhausted from libration? What did the girl do,
peering at the ruin of her good seducer,
whose rise-and-fall phenomenon
turned her on to it like opium
and left the only question in the blasted air: *More or less,*
which is to be master?

If the devil caused the flood,
he's sure to sell the sun: *I'll give you this;*

you give me that, sometime later.
So when the torrent peters into steam,

look out. *Accounts receivable.* Mushrooms
punctuate the grass, as per some ancient

fairy tale agreement. Across the street,
a stranger stops to watch your children,

son with a dandelion, daughter in a t-shirt
on her back. The way the clouds are trying to come back,

back-to-back, on her back—
there was really just a minute of that warmth

before the claim began to gather at the hairline,
dampening the brow, pulsing in the furrows,

the engrossment of a stag
stepping out of what the illustration calls the forest

to entertain his horror of the light.
He may be standing there for years, frozen in a process

of his own, in which the children figure as dilations,
the double-life of something that went wrong,

that turned around inside the cornea, and poked it
20   with the mirror-image of his horns.

What began as a delicate crack
grew wider, deeper, to become the principal
and only chasm. And there they grew,
the vegetables, peculiar to the moon, part-nerve,
part-juice, varieties of ebony
and whiteness. And to eat them,
there was life, to eat them in the sunny
lunar afternoon, to squabble over bushel prices,
contest their conical or oblong
sizes, appoint somehow a queen, a lunar beauty
to preside above the harvest boon.
But there was nothing lucky
lurking in the wet interior, sucking up
the surface plenty, a dragon infant
cutting through the skin, the soft and fragrant fats,
to reach the sweet-and-sour source
of mother, her faintly yellow labor,
quashing her, like buttercups, this thing we know
as sinister, what had to be
a terminator, a counteractive force,
to keep momenta bound to what was tangible,
to hold them down, to stop
the temperatures from rising in the bloodstream
of a pair, a true desire
that would graduate to happiness
and absolutely sail.

Floating between two nights, the heretic
can't see. His low powers of inspection
reveal a dusky streak, and it is this
he floats so far to visit, this, his own
cold streak. "Man is like a tree."
So maybe there were leaves once,
a bodily hosanna, on this
bare trunk. And maybe there was fruit,
interior vigilance (like rows and rows
of people, a fleet of them,
lighting candles for the missing);
these, the riches, risen from the roots
of a system he can't see.

He might drift into an orchard,
between two nights, and still not see
apples falling on his disbelief,
or foliage, omnipresent with rigor.
Doesn't he know this? Empty bottles,
held up to the wind, scream a solid
scream. Doesn't he know this,
that the seed is violence-bound,
so smothered by its godhead
it begets peace, or that erasure
can be full of sound, and fullness
so perverted by its burden
that it peels itself alive?

The moon makes my son go silent.
It sucks the fight from his mind,
leaving him hollow in my arms,
like a final piece of tunnel
diminished between lights.

I lose him to the brighter world;
the dark one vibrates with alarm,
as if the storm about to come
had sprung upon its axis.

Trees turn blue from drag;
leaves, like minnows, in reverse,
breaking for the shallows.
In human terms, in human terms,
their flesh is being stolen.
Long bone shadows slam into the ground.

His head is cold all over.
Its curves extend forever.
In the high winds, in the high key of heaven,
he is totally filled with God.

iii.

Thought I loved light in the morning.
Thought I loved food.

Thought I saw my son
running from a diamondback,

tears in the billions.
Still couldn't do it. Dream,

conjecture. I am the one
not shown, not pictured, not missed,

just missing. Asylum.
Leaves rolled up at the end of winter

in somebody's bowl;
loner, setting up deadfall.

Later, cassowary's girl-like screams.
Couldn't save her.

Wandering the copses
slowly. Thought I had authority.

Thought I had a stake.
Didn't know me.

I chose this. To be this
stone, grow nothing. I wanted this
absolute position in the heavens
more than anything, than you,
my two, too beautiful, my children.
A man I knew once
muttered in his terrors of the night,
no, no, no, instead of yelling.
It was this, this dismal low,
that made me leave him. I will leave them.
All the butterflies the lord above
can muster, all their roses.
I will leave whatever colors
struggle to be noticed. To leave,
to leave. That's the verb I am,
have always been, always will be,
heading, like a dewdrop,
into steamy confrontation,
my train of neutral green
lasting half a second
before casting off its freight—his arms
outside the sheet, how warm they were,
like Rome the year it burned,
Nero at the window, loving no one,
fusion crust. I fly because
my space is crossed
with fear and hair and tail and hate,
the bowels of a lioness,
iron in her roar.

Even in summer the roadside
is ghostly, patches of dry farm
like gradations of thirst,
the memoir of a woman
who became a plant: thirty-three
days without water, thirty-four,
five, a feeling of being a trillion
spinning particles, not one stream,
not one vein to any promise
of a turquoise sea. To be lost
here is to lose not just faith
in this one spot of living,
but color and texture of flesh,
as if the blood succumbed to dust
before the message to regenerate
was sent, and so the strongest
vow bows down; the eyes
that drive the arms into mirage
roll on, the steering wheel
springing from the dash, a newly
loosened bone from a swollen
body, a plumule, a radicle,
two pieces of an embryo
divided on their axis into dirt
and light, worming through
the airlessness, flying across
trellises, heading for the atrium
of heaven, or of hell, deserting
what was self, until the shoulder

circles back into the heel,
and what flashes in the rearview
are the annuals of nowhere—
begonia, low on organs, wholly
wanting snow-ball, primrose
shedding filigree and teeth.

body w/o
organs

Everything unreal is alike:
a flying turtle, a flying wife.
Whatever her needs were, unreal,
alike, extremes that touch
(the high, the low, the sickening
and burgeoning of twilight),
were those of the plague-birds,
preying on mice; whatever their needs were,
conceit, caprice, to turn to drink
or stand up straight, extremes that touch,
were hers; the same.
And whether she closed her eyes
as she entered the nebulous fetch
or extended her wild neck
(because something inside it was bright,
so bright it needed a cover),
is whether they sought the end
as they charged the deadly water,
or gloried in their liberty, in maxima,
Norwegian mice—whatever she had to do,
it must have been in raging
to leave her brood, leave her eggs unburied
with a sideways look,
see them in the jewelweed,
clean with moon, blackening with absence,
anonymous, not true.

Only the ether
is gliding above alive somewhere,

like a waft of Iceland moss,
too raw to be material.

In the not-yet world, not-yet mouths
are saying *no*,

no to color, no to a molecular
engagement to each other,

no to the infant
water's plan for webless hands,

hands that grab at once, ten digits
clamoring for land.

No to the wont of the bat,
batting the echo's madness,

the terror of what it grasps,
sound coming out of a will, will to live,

will to have.
No to the hallowed spot

that greets its prod in subsiding light,
ending the state of single life,

no that knows the hymen,
woman's dam on man,

will ease into a delta
of the blood that flows between them,

slushing into long-note sleep,
turning everything they dreamed of

back into a dream, and everything they'd been,
forward into being

nothing more than what they were as seeds,
spores of the sporangia

clinging to the veinwork,
loyal to the forks that subdivide

and never meet.
And that's why their inheritance,

this nullifying genesis,
this *yes* which is an ornament of no,

opens, like a peacock,
for everyone but them to see.

negation

affirmation

Did you hear, *I heard,*
that I flew, *you flew,*
at dusk, like the foxes,
my eyes, *your eyes,*
silver-white, like foxes,
and flew, *you flew,*
over things, *what things,*
in there, *in where,*
the trees, *what trees,*
reached up, *reached what,*
for me, my fur,
your fur, I heard,
they pulled, *pulled what,*
our love, *a ruse,*
was rare, on earth,
like stars that fall,
like ice, and spread,
spread what, my legs,
your legs, were white,
silver-white, like ice,
and shook, *shook what,*
my heart, *what heart,*
in truth, our love,
a ruse, on earth,
was caught, *by what,*
by things, *what things,*
my tongue, *your tongue,*
was white, *silver-white,*
like leaves, and split,
split what, in two,

like ghosts, at dusk,
like wings, *they whisht*,
not hurt, in truth,
just lost, *a ruse*.

Somewhere along the rim
of midnight-altered water,
a strange new glow coats the fish
that weave in and out of the nutrient murk
like bleeding rubies, making it seem
that the heron pulling them out
is pulling a long and desperate feeling—
the longing of water for fish,
the longing one has to give, to attach,
to keep hurting. To keep pulling out
what is wrong, skin too hot
to be good, unable to stop
the feeling of not being full,
of wanting more tail in the throat
to weave its way through, pulling until
the feeling of pulling is gone
and longingness burns the heron,
until nothing familiar remains,
pulling, bleeding. That's when the anger
reflex of trees lets go of the wind
for a dream of rest, and everything torn
from home, from flesh, morass,
bones and joints and noise, floats up
into the still cosmogony of night
where the wish to live disappears
in a surgery that lasts.

There are light and milk and worship
on us all, which is why
I don't mind if she's spotted.
Hills are just plains
that rose in disobedience,
how long can you hold your anger,
blanched with latent purity,
bowed back down,
the way breasts ask forgiveness of the body
for being supernatant,
cowering, when all the mouths are done.
Twins are the way
love fell through me twice,
so I fix them to her udder
like slow-chewing fire. Which is why
I don't mind. Go,
if you're furious with women.
Go and do some rising. Milk is the proof
that what we disturb
in turn disturbs beautifully,
clearing the moon like a ruminant martyr.

A father lost in the clouds.
A mother and son
toughing it out together;
their quarrel, her tossing

out the window of beans,
his beautiful things
of no street value.
During the night they sprout.

By dawn he's over the sky,
crossing a moat to a giant's castle;
father inside with a harp,
something like love going on,

a niagara of grappling sounds.
The giant is calling the shots:
Pluck here, pluck there.
Jack drops to the floor,

transformed by joy into lather.
Mother below grows tired.
Where is the gold-laying hen?
When is the family reunion?

Beanstalk fuming with drab.
God rot. She punches the base,
lops off the vein
to their faraway songs with an axe.

iv.

When there is no more life,
step outside. Peel away the human.

becoming animal

If the sky can't keep an opening,
be the opening

that ushers in the dusk
that masquerades the nothingness

with arteries of color,
the swell and swerve of nervous

wrecks, their kamikaze
shadows. Be that symbol

of the lost but well-fought war,
the bandage on the side effect,

not the real sore, of thousand-mile
bitternesses crossed by geese

against the odds of snow
until what binds them to repeat

themselves dissolves,
muscles, wings, and throats

twisting like grotesques
of ice, their inner water, in a flux,

indentured to the half
they didn't know, like galaxies,

accessories, before the fact,
drawn into the power of a hole.

Their throats are bursting
with the depth and power of the night,
the increasing need for release
as they lope through a lull in the snow
that turns into rain on their fur,
the same that rained on their beginnings,
waters of mothers filling them up,
the way numbers fill music
and spectra, controlling the flesh
with flowing aggression,
the wolves in the rain of their making
already whet by the moon,
her evasion, her underneath longing to die,
to blot out the light from the root
of their name and stop all this crying
to her, these ritual songs,
exhibited mouths that foam at the seams
from the strain of their tongues
whose buds, come spring, are done in
by famine: a peregrine tone,
a transparent unguent, a soul
on the floor of a womb.

The world is mortal.
Its parts are mortal.
The beach is in summer form.

A girl I know is falling
out of favor, like a toy,
falling out of harmony, of e's

and i's, almost barking,
August, come. She cannot hear
the cause of her dismissal,

cannot hear the god
(no reception in the Sylvian,
the fissure), the softening

of gyri, poverty of fibers
and possesses, cannot hear
herself, lying by herself

at the bottom of the cochlea,
whitening with time, mistaking it
for touch, imagining she's still

her father's favorite, whitening
too much, a sheer veneer
badgered by interiors,

like a child who did not thrive,
the spine, the cause, the god,
tossing in the bora's bawdy sound,

deaf to the great wet gasps
she doesn't recognize as mother's
(whose promises of rest

are breaking now, were broken then,
breaking up the daughter's shell,
beating on the tympani,

scooping out her meatus)—
cannot hear, *August, gone,*
the counter-counter-pieces.

Everything has its time, even once.
When it's gone, say good-bye.
When it has not yet come, sit it out.
Once, in the joy of a thaw, the moths flew up and died.
That was their triumph. They killed winter.
And you, what did you kill when you died?
The gene for survival. Good-bye.
In their brief dusk, the moths had looked down
and seen that the world wasn't round
or azure, but *they* were, and like destination
in a palm, could exercise the outcome
if their silhouettes were constant,
rotation, counterclockwise, reversing the old score
(the half-push, the half-door, the half-light),
and you could almost make them out,
they were almost alike, synching in their free fall
like a pair of dice, to settle on the shrapnel
of an oyster shell, a glowing one,
a loaded one, a mother, with a daughter,
with a finger, who'd been pried.

If blood were clear, the *viol*
of violation would be sounded—
not the fear—and how it landed,
in a pool or spray, would change
the sound, not the color, of the floor
by being clear. The *viol*
would go the way of music,
not of fear, the sound of staying
whole, not of being blasted.
If blood were clear, the *viol*
would slide right out of the clothes,
out of the uniform of mental
holdings, out of the bow. Out
to attract more solid world
happenings, attract, like sound,
by passing through, leaving longing
on the surface like a shadow
or a word. The people in the score,
for trio or quartet, are often
strangers. Here they know each other
well, the one who falls, the one
who fells her, *d'amore, da braccio,*
and their *figli.* If blood were clear,
and she were heavy, heavily,
like sirens, it would flow, sirens
in the yellow morning thunder,
sirening discovery, incendiary, loss
of self-control; if she were light,
and blood were clear, the sound
of smoke, of silent silent o's,

the save-me signals of a soldier
whose mind is still at war,
the silent snap of crayfish,
the hardest range for the *viol*.
If blood were clear, and flying
into sunset, propelled by strings
of the *viol*, the sound of happy
ending would be visible,
but somewhere else, not here
where blood is blood offstage—
these two boys, all eyes and ears,
sitting up too straight,
burgundy with noise.

PATHOGEN

Is it diabolic,
floating through the family
like a moonlit seed,
infinitesimal and hungry,
to eat the golden pieces of their beauty,
the special energies that mingle in their skin,
to cut and thrust, then toss the rest
like water, the interior of father in a stream,
trailing vortices of daughter
like a baby leopard seal, oceanic *no*
from cresting mother, *whoever did this*,
the route of invasion, every direction,
forcing them to spiral in defense,
to spread apart, like antlers, on the ceiling
of nonlife, not feel itself, the family,
carried out of sight, beyond the spectrum,
beyond echo, vanished by a thing
they couldn't see, like ghostly ships
with inner jibs the early people couldn't see,
the fore-and-aft, the furrowed shore
that warned them with recoil, *run*,
but still they couldn't see, the countenance
that hovered at the bow,
the volume of the eye behind the scope,
the way it held them in its pale
and closed.

Wooded area has wed itself
to crime, and sometimes *alley*
binds with molestation, and then a tiny clue,
the treadmark of a shoe, yarn hair
of a doll, will carry on the language
like a fossil, *shallow grave,*
the way a hoofprint of a mammal with four toes
broadens the whole epoch of the horse,
connecting time and place and suspect
in a brand-new constellation.

The chief detective starts to find them:
sidelong angle of a neck
suggesting one-way struggle,
like surrender to an ancient warrior
or athlete, what Greeks might call
gorgeous boy with javelin;
dandruff on the welcome mat
with matching DNA . . .

A *fall* comes burning down from heaven,
a meteor, an iron, pounding the young corn
in this or that dark county.
A fall is classified as actual
and named for where it fell—*Gallup,*
Petaluma, Kettering.

A *find* is just the fall
unwitnessed. A find is picked up later.
We take the finder's word for it,

but reserve a little room for doubt.
We test the find. We put the finder
in the line-up, in a row of men
who stare beyond the viewing lens
like otherworldly musicians.

Glass divides the witness from the pederasts.
The notes she hears are streaming from their hands,
impossible to cipher, bamboo snares
that pluck a tiny wing, then softly play the body
that is lying still, *piano, piano,*
so as not to rouse the consciousness,

but let it linger in its wilt,
the wounded bird, half-asleep,
returning to a paradise, free of all taxonomy,
of narrow paths, of artifacts—
of water-bearers and their centaurs
in a midnight saturnalia.

THE UNFORESEEN

I.

All trees move
at all times
to all music,

cypress, sequoia,
Don Giovanni,
three in the morning,

Hush-a-bye baby,
floorboards creaking,
a boy still lost

in his dream
with an airplane,
a man in the window,

respira, o cara,
when the wind blows,
come mi fa terror.

II.

And the cave was therein,
and they entered to hide
the silver. And they cried when they saw
she was dead. Because no one

wants things, not really,
not for themselves. Not for themselves,
the shine on her crown,
not for themselves, her limbs bent low
in the river, Adda, the river,
the capture, themselves. And they wanted
to run with all of their might,
like dogs in a field with children,
all of their breath coming out,
all of their come, all of their wine,
the lie to themselves, *come, come,*
a continuous diamond.

III.

See how the water adjusts
to the slap on its face,

its chloroform stare
at home with the flogging

stars, like the girl in the tower
named after rapine

who knew all along
there was nothing around

but blood, that blood is just water
turned red, red with desire,

the failure to love.
So she let it all down,

molecules, truths,
eternal golden strands,

holding on to phantasms,
the way you hold your paddle

and pole, taking your time,
over and under, the witch almost up,

the fish full of hook, its loosening
lips, like news that stuns.

If it has flown, then it knows
God tore the world,
and the space between heaven and earth
is in shreds, and the question of living
deep in the hollering sun,
or homing the spas near heaven,
or living at all, not wanting to live
on earth as it is, is tense.

And if it has flown, it has peered
down at the thing called rock, and felt stilled
by the rock's longevity, and has flown
with a fear in its eye of longevity,
peering again, asking, *Why, God, is it still*,
closing the eye and feeling divided,
like the flying lizard of myth,
cut off, afloat, doffing skin after skin,
a Jerusalem heart, exposed.

THE IOWA POETRY PRIZE & EDWIN FORD PIPER POETRY AWARD WINNERS

1987
Elton Glaser, *Tropical Depressions*
Michael Pettit, *Cardinal Points*

1988
Bill Knott, *Outremer*
Mary Ruefle, *The Adamant*

1989
Conrad Hilberry, *Sorting the Smoke*
Terese Svoboda, *Laughing Africa*

1990
Philip Dacey,
    Night Shift at the Crucifix Factory
Lynda Hull, *Star Ledger*

Greg Pape, *Sunflower Facing the Sun*
Walter Pavlich,
    Running near the End of the World

1992
Lola Haskins, *Hunger*
Katherine Soniat, *A Shared Life*

1993
Tom Andrews,
    The Hemophiliac's Motorcycle
Michael Heffernan, *Love's Answer*
John Wood, *In Primary Light*

1994
James McKean, *Tree of Heaven*
Bin Ramke, *Massacre of the Innocents*
Ed Roberson,
    Voices Cast Out to Talk Us In

1995
Ralph Burns, *Swamp Candles*
Maureen Seaton, *Furious Cooking*

1996
Pamela Alexander, *Inland*
Gary Gildner,
    The Bunker in the Parsley Fields
John Wood,
    The Gates of the Elect Kingdom

1997
Brendan Galvin, *Hotel Malabar*
Leslie Ullman, *Slow Work through Sand*

1998
Kathleen Peirce, *The Oval Hour*
Bin Ramke, *Wake*
Cole Swensen, *Try*

1999
Larissa Szporluk, *Isolato*
Liz Waldner,
    A Point Is That Which Has No Part